BROWN GIRLS GUIDE TO EMPLOYMENT AND NETWORKING

By Dr. Tamika Jacques

Dedicated To My Original Brown Girls – KJ & IJ

Contents

Introduction 3

Chapter One 5

Who Are You? 5

Career Inventory Tests 7

Your Resume 11

Chapter Two 13

Where Do You Start? 13

Professional Organizations 13

Networking 17

Attending Events 19

• When You Should Arrive............................. 19

• Where You Should Sit................................. 21

• Using Business Cards.................................. 22

• When You Should Leave............................... 23

• Following Up.. 24

Chapter Three 27

Referrals and Interviews 27

Unofficial Interviews vs. Official Interviews................ 27

Internships... 30

Career Transitions.. 32

The Importance of Compensation.................... 33

Reward Yourself (Vacation, Sick & Personal Days)......36

Chapter Four 39

Final Thoughts & Tips 39

Diversifying Your Network 39

Feeling Good About Yourself......................... 40

Paying It Forward... 41

You Got This!.. 42

Network with Me!... 43

Introduction

Hey, Beautiful Brown Girl! You are reading this because you are seeking new employment, either at a new company or organization or within your current company or organization. First, I want you to know that, as brown girls, we come from a long line of ancestors who, when the world told them no, said "yes." Don't get discouraged if your job search is taking longer than you prefer. What you want to do is remain positive and know that your "no" will turn into a "yes." You will find your dream job!

The reason I wrote this guide is because I have been helping job seekers navigate their employment journey for the past eighteen years while navigating my own employment journey at the same time. The tips and advice in this guide are simply tips I wished someone had given me before I decided to accept a job offer. I want you to learn from my mistakes. I want you to be able to turn them into opportunities that will help you land your dream job or work in your dream industry. I want you to reach your highest potential.

Chapter One

Who Are You?

The first step in preparing yourself to read this guide is to ask yourself, "Where do I truly see myself?" If you are struggling with this question, now is the time to invest in taking a career inventory test to better understand your interests and where your focus should be. If you have an idea of the industry you want to join, a career inventory test will also help you better understand how you will fit into your industry of choice and the types of environments that will best suit your character. Most career inventory tests are free. If you want to understand more about your traits and characteristics or need a deeper dive, then the test you choose might require you to pay additional fees.

Reflection:
Where do I truly see myself?

_____

_____

_____

_____

_____

_____

_____

_____

_____

_____

_____

_____

_____

_____

_____

_____

_____

_____

Career Inventory Tests

A career inventory test is an assessment based on your preferences of how you interact with others, the type of tasks you like or dislike, and the environments you prefer to work in. The outcome of this type of test can lead you in the right direction toward the types of career environments and tasks that will most likely make you happiest while on your career journey. While these tests are not always 100% accurate, they give you a good indication of where you should start in your career journey. In fact, taking such a test before reading this guide will open your mind to new career ideas and opportunities. As you read the guide, it is important to keep your career vision in mind.

If you are a believer in God and are currently serving in a church ministry, you probably have been asked to take what is called a "gift test." This type of test can also lead you to identify what industry you should focus on. Career inventory tests and gift tests will help you find your purpose and destiny. This can lead you to want to get up and go to work each day, rather than grumbling about having to wake up and go to a place that makes you miserable. Once you have done a career inventory test, you can start thinking about the foundations of your career and start to dream bigger. Then you can understand what steps it will take to get to your greatest potential and where you feel you will be most successful.

Just what is your greatest potential? Remember, only you can define what that is and it is continually evolving. For example, one person's greatest potential might be reached through a career path that leads them to start their own business, another person's through a career path that leads to being a CEO of a non-profit organization, or another's through a career path that allows them to pay off all their debt and build wealth so they can become a philanthropist. No matter how you define your greatest potential, you are the only one who can write and define the definition and the only one who can add and change the definition when needed. This guide is meant to give you tips on how to achieve your greatest potential for the entire length of your career history.

Reflection:

What did my career inventory test indicate? Any Surprises?

_____

_____

_____

_____

_____

_____

_____

_____

_____

_____

_____

_____

_____

_____

_____

_____

Cut and paste pictures of what reflects your dream job. When you get discouraged keep looking at this page.

Your Resume

This is the only section of this guide that will discuss the importance of having an effective resume. While an error-free and well-developed resume is important, I personally don't think it is the only thing that will lead you to a successful career path. It is just one piece of the successful employment puzzle. You should look at and revise your resume every six months.

Job responsibilities can change in an instant, and it's important that you describe the story of what you do when job duties change. It's easier to update your resume at your own "will" than to have someone ask, "Do you have a resume?" When this happens, you have to rush home and summarize all you have achieved as quickly as you can because someone on the other end is waiting to hear back from you. That kind of haste is not going to help you achieve your greatest career potential. Your greatest career potential is going to be achieved if your resume is always ready when the next opportunity arrives.

If you have attended a higher education institution, usually the institution will allow you to use their career center for *free* and get assistance with your resume. This is called an alumni benefit. You paid the price to attend, so you should use the career service center when you feel the need. If you have not attended post-secondary education or vocational training, your state has government funded career centers that will help job seekers for *free*. For example, Massachusetts has thirty-two career centers located around the state. These centers have professionals that specialize in resume writing, interviewing, and other services to help with the pursuit of finding successful employment. If you have extra coins lying around and don't live near your higher-education institution, hire a professional resume writer or job coach who can assist you with your resume and help you practice interviewing.

A sharp resume will display your gifts and talent on paper and show the accomplishments that have taken place during your career because of those great gifts and talents. As mentioned earlier, a resume is just one part of securing a successful career. The next steps in this guide contain the other puzzle pieces that will get you onto your successful career path.

Chapter Two

Where Do You Start?

Professional Organizations

The first part of this guide mentions the discovery of your interests, talents, and pursuits based on the findings from a career inventory or "gift" test. Once you have the outcomes of your test, it is now time to research what opportunities and jobs are focused around those outcomes or the specific talents and skills that you possess. Your first step is to research professional organizations that represent the industry that you want to join. The goal is to meet and join others who share the same types of outcomes from the same career test or others who share similar career interests. Professional organizations help you see the viewpoint of the industry you want to join through different perspectives and opinions. The websites of professional organizations contain newsletters, current news that is happening in the industry, employment postings, events, and other opportunities that are available to members and non-members. From your research, you should be able to discover how many events per year they organize, who is part of their membership, the cost to attend their events if you are a member or a non-member, or how can you get involved with the organization. If you are seeking a leadership opportunity, then think about joining organizations that will allow you to become a member and join a committee or even lead a committee. Also, if you have a certain skill or talent, some associations might let you barter your services for a *free* membership. For example, if you do photography on the side, then you can take pictures at their event, or, if you possess writing skills, you can write a blog post or write an article on their webpage. Let your skills, talents, and hobbies work for you.

Once you research and join the professional organization, you should commit to attending one event they are hosting each month if you are a job seeker. If you are not a job seeker, then commit to attending every other month. The goal is to grow your professional contact list whether you are employed or not employed. The mistake people often make is that, once they find a job, they stop attending networking events or think they don't need that association anymore. You actually will need the association more once you land your dream job so that you are constantly keeping old connections and new connections aware of your current position and how you are using your skills and talents. We should all be on a continuous learning path to meet new people, discover what they do, and collaborate with them when needed. If the contacts in your network consist only of people inside your company or your family members, this will not help you discover what other types of opportunities are within your dream industry or meet other women and men who are having successful careers.

If you decide to join a professional organization that is identity-based (i.e.: based on race or gender), that is fine; you should also join or attend another organization that focuses more on topics, challenges, and successes of the industry. For example, if you join an organization such as the American Association of Blacks in Energy, then also join an organization for women in energy and another organization that is just focused on the entire energy industry.

I recommend joining three organizations. Choose three that seem to fit the type of interests you want to pursue. Most organizations will require you to become a member to actively participate. Some will allow you to interact with their organization by not paying an upfront membership fee, but you probably will have to pay per event or meeting you attend. How you decide to interact with each organization is up to you. Your career needs will determine your level of interaction with the organization. If you find yourself still undecided on what industry to join or pursue, you may not want to become a member; instead, you may just want to be part of their email list. If you are looking for employment in your current industry and not seeking an industry change, I encourage you to join a professional organization. Once you have attained successful employment, you want to be up-to-date on the trends of the industry.

So, you have researched your professional organizations, and you have joined. What is your next step? The next step is to become active in your professional organization. Attend events, panel discussions or industry-sponsored events to meet others who have your interests. It's called "networking."

Networking

When you saw the word "networking", how did you react? When I discuss networking, most women have one of two feelings: they either "love it" or "hate it". You can drop the people who love it into the middle of a room with eighty people, and they interject themselves into different conversations, introduce themselves, boast about themselves and the type of job they have, remain memorable to the people they talk with, and then walk away with a minimum of ten business cards. They often give testimonies about how they landed their dream job from meeting someone at an event. These types of women have extrovert characteristics.

The people who "hate it" probably made a face when they saw the word "networking." When you drop these folks into a room with eighty people, they run to the first person they know, or they look for people that look exactly like them (similar skin color, same attire, etc.), or they sit in a corner and play on their phone the whole night. They simply do not know how to engage or are not comfortable to "network" with others.

Twenty years ago, you probably could have landed a job without networking. However, because the world is constantly changing, sending your resume and waiting for a business or organization to call you for an interview is simply not enough today. You must network or learn how to network.

Payscale.com suggests that 85% of open positions are filled through networking.[1]

If you are going to find your dream job, you are going to have to network your way through an industry so that, at some point, you can pass along that resume that is already waiting for the next opportunity. So how do you do this? How can you get rid of the anxiety associated with networking? The following tips will guide you to feeling more confident when you network and attend events.

---

[1] https://www.payscale.com/career-news/2017/04/many-jobs-found-networking

Attending Events

When You Should Arrive

- Arrive ten-to-fifteen minutes early if no designated time for mingling with others is listed on the agenda.
- Commit to leaving your phone in your purse, not checking email, or using any apps for a minimum of thirty minutes.

By arriving early, you force yourself to talk with others who you don't know, mingle with others who are in the industry you want to join, and meet individuals who may not look like you but who want to meet new people, whether they are in your industry or not. Do you need help starting a conversation? Use simple topics about current industry trends or discuss the atmosphere of the event you are attending. The goal is to meet new people from all walks of life. Arriving late to events often means you have to sit in the back of the room, stand up longer than needed, or be uncomfortable because your feet start to hurt in the five-inch heels you are wearing. Late attendance also means that you come in after small groups have been formed. It can benefit you to be in a small group. The larger a group gets, the harder it may become for you to speak up and get to know others because several conversations can be happening at once. If you're late, you might not have the time to introduce yourself to others because the event is starting.

Networking is deliberate and arriving early allows you to deliberately meet at least one person, despite any anxiety you might be feeling. Leaving your phone in your purse for thirty minutes forces you to mingle and keep your head up. People then assume from your body language that you are interested in meeting others. When your head is down in your phone, it shows others that you are not interested in starting new conversations and that, at that moment, email or social media are more important than meeting others in the room. It is important that your body language suggests you are open to meeting and learning about the career paths of others in the industry.

Where You Should Sit

You should strategically place yourself in a middle seat or middle row when attending events with seated venues. For events that have chairs, do not sit on the end of a row, in the back row, or in the front row. Sit in the middle rows, so you will have the opportunity to turn around to the front or the back of you. You want to have one person on your right, one person on your left, and possibly a few people in front of you or behind you. Strategically sitting in the middle rows will force others to speak to you, and this will help if you do not want to start conversations yourself.

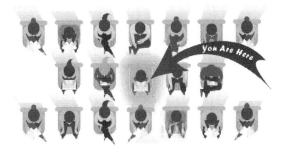

Most events give name tags. Feel free to play coy and look at someone's name tag so you can start a conversation based on learning their name, their company, or the industry they represent.

Using Business Cards

Networking can happen any time or any place, and it can be unplanned or planned. If you are employed, your company most likely provides business cards, and you must keep them in your wallet at all times. If you are employed and your company does not provide business cards, make your own. There are online printing companies that make business cards for little cost. If you are seeking other opportunities and do not want to use your current business card, create your own card. List the types of skills or talent you possess and the types of projects you have worked on or are seeking. You design your own business card based on your preferences. For example, your business card might include a picture of you or the address of your LinkedIn handle that leads to a more in-depth description of what you have accomplished. These types of business cards are great if you are seeking to transition from one industry to another or to another employer. See sample below.

When You Should Leave

Don't be the first to leave at the end of the event! Stick around a few minutes to mingle, meet featured panelists, or meet the coordinators of the event. This will help you make direct connections or even sign up to volunteer at the next event. It is important that, by the time you leave an event, you have met and introduced yourself to a minimum of two people and have collected a minimum of three business cards.

Following Up

Now that you understand how to engage with others, it is important to follow-up with the people that you have engaged with. Networking follow-up is important, and I strongly encourage you to do it within forty-eight hours of meeting an individual. First, if you exchanged or collected someone's business card, write on the back of the card something you can remember about them or the conversation. It's helpful to write where you met them, the date, the topic of your conversation, and maybe something you admired most about them. Then within forty-eight hours send them a follow-up email mentioning how you enjoyed your conversation, how you look forward to connecting with them again in the future, and that you hope to see them at the next event.

Perhaps the business card is from someone you would like to learn more about because their career path or the type of job they are currently in is of special interest to you. If this is the case, then ask in the email if they would mind meeting for a thirty-minute coffee or hour-long lunch so they can discuss in further detail what their job entails and how they navigated into their career path. When you meet with them for coffee or lunch, it is important to have your listening ears on, so you can benefit from what they are saying and their words of advice.

Most people do not have a lot of time so come prepared with questions. Here are some examples. 1) When did you know you wanted to join this industry? 2) What is the most challenging part of the industry? 3) How can I work my way up to get to where I want to be in this industry? It is important that you are honest about where you are in your career path, what you would like your next position to be, and the type of career environment you might be interested in joining. After you have talked about your interests, ask if the person has heard about any job openings or individuals or companies that are seeking the type of talent you possess. If they say no at this time, that is ok. Just ask if they might be able to refer you to two other people who are part of the industry. You should not assume that everyone is going to be able to know of open job positions or lead you in the correct direction. Still, you should assume that they will be able to refer you to at least two other people who will lead you closer to your dream job. Asking everyone you network with to introduce you to two people will help you gain insight into where you want to be in your employment and where you do not want to be in your next job position. Eventually you will hear of companies or industry professionals who are looking to hire someone like you. If you follow these exact steps, you will have met and networked with at least three people who will have given you advice on how to find your next dream job. It's important not to stop at three people, though. Take your time.

Keep going out and getting referred to new people. Think about the advice that each person gave you as well as the next steps you should pursue before you decide to have another conversation with an industry professional. Challenge yourself to meet and get referrals until you gain the type of employment that you know will help you reach your highest potential. The key is to be patient and not be in a rush to find your next place of employment.

The last point about following up is to be sure to update the people you have met with on your progress. Remember to thank them for their referral. Let them know that you have met with their referral and the direction that person has pointed you in. People love to know that you are following their advice, and its helps to keep your name fresh in their mind.

Chapter Three

Referrals and Interviews

Unofficial Interviews vs. Official Interviews

As you are meeting new people you've been referred to, it is important to remember that people you meet with could one day be your boss, a colleague you have to work with, or a client you have to work for. Consider a referral meet-and-greet as an unofficial interview. Just as you are learning about their background, they also are learning about yours, so it's important to remain positive during a meet-and-greet or lunch meeting. I am not saying to not be yourself during a meet-and-greet, be aware that you also are being interviewed. Do not expose all your career business. For example, I discussed how you should take a career inventory test and learn about the type of environments you prefer. I encourage you to feel free to discuss your learning from your career inventory test. What you should not discuss are the types of people or specific colleagues or supervisors that you simply did not get along with. Remember to stay positive and focus on the larger picture of how your talent will shape your career endeavors. After you have developed a colleague relationship with the person you are networking with, you might find it appropriate to divulge personal career information. Remember, not everyone is your best friend. Some industries are cut-throat and competitive, so you don't want to discuss personal information that may at some point be used against you in your career. I feel strongly about this tip. Depending on the industry you join, it may seem like a vast industry. Yet, when the industry gets broken down into different sectors, it becomes small. Usually someone knows someone, and people do communicate with each other. Chances are they will remember if you talked negatively about an employer or someone they know.

The same approach should be taken when on an official interview. Do not discuss personal career business that is not positive. Again, do not discuss co-workers who were not so nice to you or employers you did not enjoy working for. Instead, come prepared to the interview understanding the key points about the organization (number of employees, goals or strategic plan, information about the department you want to join, etc.). Questions that they may ask might include: 1) Why do you want to join this company? 2) How do you prioritize tasks under pressure? 3) What are the skills that you can bring to the organization?

Questions you should ask include 1) Describe the company culture. 2) What is a common misconception that people you supervise think of you? 3) What is a common misconception that others think of this division?

You will never know all the questions that will be asked of you on an interview. The key is to be confident when answering the questions. Your confidence will be boosted the more you come prepared to the interview. You should treat an interview for an internship the same way that you prepare for an official interview for full-time employment. Always be prepared!

Internships

If you have spare time, consider an internship or a hands-on learning experience. I encourage you to seek this type of opportunity. The importance of an internship is that it helps you gain critical experience and also helps you discover what types of career environments you prefer.

If you are a college student, I encourage you to commit to one internship before you graduate. An internship will save you the future pain of having to be in a job that you dislike for any length of time. Being in a job that you dislike for more than one day already means you have been there too long! An internship is for a defined period of time, usually between three and six months. You are given specific duties and tasks to complete during your stay at the company. It is important when you go on an interview for an internship that you ask the interviewer or hiring manager what skill or skills you will learn by the end of your defined time at the company. If an employer can not define what you will gain at the end of the internship, you should be on high alert that the internship probably will not be a valuable experience. In every internship you should be a benefit to the employer, and what you learn should also benefit you. Internship postings can be found at your college career services office or inquiring from your professor or faculty advisor.

During your defined stay at your internship, you will also find out the type of job environment you prefer. You may need engagement with colleagues all day and prefer a team environment, or you may prefer an environment where you have little interaction with colleagues or only interact with them in a staff meeting. An internship will help you learn and decide what type of environment (fast paced, slow, quiet, loud, team style, etc.) that you need for succeeding in a dream job. Finally, at the end of your internship, do your own self-evaluation. Ask yourself these questions: 1) Do I see myself in this industry for the next five years? 2) Is this the type of industry that will keep me stimulated and allow me to be innovative while using my talent and skills? 3) Is there enough room in this industry so that I can move around if I choose to be a manager, senior vice president, or chief operating officer or even start my own company? The objective is to think beyond the internship and envision yourself rising to the top of whatever industry you choose.

Career Transitions

If you are in in a career transition and can only give a few hours per week to a hands-on learning experience, you will have to be more creative. You are going to have to network your way around and find someone who will let you do a "job shadow" when time allows. I would suggest you volunteer at an organization that has a volunteer position that is similar to the type of job you'd want to get paid to perform. Volunteering is often done when your time permits, so you can put as little or as much time as you wish into gaining relevant experience and increasing your skill set. Consider joining a non-profit board that represents something you have a passion for, so you can use your talents and enjoy the experience while you are volunteering your time. These experiences can then be put on your resume and will be a talking point for a future interview or a talking point for a future coffee or lunch meeting with a contact.

See sample below.

<u>*Animal Rescue Group, Boston, MA*</u>
2016 – Present

Volunteer Board Member/Event Photographer
- Attend meetings and make administrative decisions
- Serve as the event photographer for all fundraising events
- Edit and photoshop photos that are sold on webpage to raise money for all administrative costs

The Importance of Compensation

At this point, you have thought about the tips in the guide and can even see yourself using the tips to gain successful employment. Once you navigate through your employment process and have job offers you need to understand your whole salary and what it will mean to your lifestyle. I often speak with job seekers to find out why they are ready to move on so quickly from a job they just started and love. Most career guides do not talk about this. Usually, it is because there is no opportunity for their economic growth. In simpler terms, they need more money to be able to live from day-to-day. When you find your dream job and look at the compensation that is being offered, it is important that you figure out what your base salary includes and the deductions that will be taken out of your paycheck. These are based on your tax bracket, which depends on how much you make. For example, if your base salary is $50,000 per year and you have deductions (such as for health insurance, etc.) that total $5,000 per year, you are left with a base salary of $45,000. From the $45,000 the Federal government could take up to an additional 25% for taxes, so that leaves you with a base of $33,750. State tax deductions will vary depending on where you live. You need to ask yourself if you can live on the after-tax salary and still pay your rent, mortgage, transportation costs, and other living expenses. It is important to understand whether accepting a salary of $50,000 before taxes is going to allow you to enjoy your dream job without requiring you to get a second job. Your goal is to feel happy in your employment without having to think about finding another place of employment because of your financial situation. There are several free budget and salary applications for your smartphone. Do a google search and do the one that is comfortable for you and includes the cost of living adjustments for the state you live in. For example, someone who lives in Massachusetts probably needs more funds for rent or mortgage verses the person who lives in North Carolina.

As part of your budget calculations, do not forget to allocate funds to your retirement. If your company has a matching retirement plan, use it. If they do not, a small dollar amount from your salary is better than not putting away anything at all. Part of having a successful career is planning for your future.

Dr. Tamika Jacques

Sample Bi-Weekly Pay Statement

Pay Statement

Date:	December 28, 2018
Statement #	24

		Bi-WEEKLY	YEAR
Gross Pay		$1,923.00	$50,000.00
Deductions			
	Federal Income Tax	$211.00	$5,486.00
	MA State Income Tax	$98.00	$2,548.00
	Retirement (401)	$98.00	$2,548.00
Other			
	Dental	$10.00	$260.00
	Medical	$160.00	$4,160.00
	Vision	$15.00	$390.00
NET PAY		$1,331.00	$34,608.00

Based on two paychecks per month. Two months out of the year you might have three pay statements (bi-weekly).

Sample Expense Sheet

Expense Sheet

		MONTHLY COST	YEARLY COST
		$2,662.00	$37,154.00
		(Take Home Pay)	(Take Home Pay)
	Car Payment	$400.00	$4,800.00
	Car Insurance	$83.00	$2,000.00
	Rent	$1,200.00	$14,400.00
	Food	$200.00	$3,600.00
	Savings	$384.00	$2,304.00
	Charitable Contribution	$384.00	$2,304.00
	Student Loans	$150.00	$1,800.00
Total Expenses		$2,801.00	$31,208.00
Disposable Income Per Month/Year		$139.00	$5,946.00

Reward Yourself (Vacation, Sick & Personal Days)

When you figure out the financial part of your compensation, the next step is to think about how you will reward yourself for your hard work and accomplishments. Compensation is not only financial. Think about how you will celebrate your career accomplishments. Celebrating accomplishments and planning for unforeseen circumstances translates into vacation, sick days, and personal days. Negotiation of these days will be explained in the next guide, Volume 2. For now, it is important that your dream job include these "accomplishment days."

Vacation days give you rejuvenation time after you have worked hard and committed yourself to your place of employment. Rejuvenation allows you to celebrate yourself and reflect on your career journey. I want you to celebrate your career accomplishments every six months because you are a phenomenal woman! Maybe you cannot afford to take a full vacation. If not, then take at least one vacation day to sit by the beach, eat at your favorite restaurant, or use the day to catch up with your girlfriends. The point is to reward yourself for your career accomplishments with something that you consider a treat.

Sick days are needed because our bodies do get run down from time-to-time. If you are a mom, you know what happens when your child is sick. You usually come down with the same symptoms right after your child does. Personal days are also needed because you need to be able to handle unforeseen circumstances or personal business and attend to emergencies without the stress of Wondering whether you will get paid for missing a day of work.

I understand some professions only hire contractors, so the option of having included vacation, sick days, and personal days will not be part of your compensation package. I want you to still find a way to celebrate career accomplishments. Prepare financially for vacation days and even sick days. Create a separate account to save for vacation or days when you are sick or have an emergency. Plan for important time off that you will need. Preparation is key.

Chapter Four

Final Thoughts & Tips

Diversifying Your Network

When you go to a professional networking event, be aware of yourself and make sure you make an effort to have a diverse network. Often as brown girls we tend to network with people who only look like us. Yes, you should network with other brown girls. After all, you are reading this guide, so I know you can relate with other brown girls. Still, the key to effective networking is to have a diverse network of people who don't necessarily look like you and who don't always think like you yet who are in the industry you desire to join.

Feeling Good About Yourself

Following the suggestions in this guide will be easy for some and more difficult for others. Either way, it will cause you to open up to sharing who you are and what you have accomplished. As women we should all have an invisible security blanket. No one will see it, yet we know that it's there making us feel secure. Fox example, when I have on a new pair of undergarments, I feel confident because of how they make me feel. I even have a pair that says "Good Vibes" going around the waist. Maybe you feel confident or unstoppable when you wear your grandma's necklace. Whatever your security blanket is, you should wear it when you go to a networking event or on an interview. You will feel secure and confident because of the reminder that only you can see.

I would like to remind you that, once you have found successful employment, you have to continue with all of the steps in this guide. At some point in your career, it will be time again for another career shift. You want to make sure you are prepared no matter what point you are in your career path.

Paying It Forward

As you go through your employment process and then successfully gain employment, you must never forget the people you met with, who encouraged you, and who helped you find your dream job or industry. You must always take the opportunity to meet with job seekers who are seeking your advice. Always look for the new face in the room when you attend an event so that you can make newcomers feel comfortable. Guide another woman into her dream job or dream industry. Be open to speaking on panels so you can encourage not just one person but a whole audience by sharing your story. Remember you are a role model and can become a mentor and personal role model to other women and men in your industry. Your career story is important, and others need to hear about your great accomplishments!

You Got This!

You are the only one that can define your greatest potential! As you mature through your career path you will better understand yourself and what type of job or industry will define your greatest potential. At some point in your career path, maybe you find yourself successful yet yearning for more, again you are the only one that can define the "more". I encourage you to write out the "more job description", the exact way you envision yourself doing the job and how it will be carried out. If more ladies would write our own job description, then focus and set goals toward achieving the "more", we would have more women led businesses. Instead we would be working for ourselves in a job description that perfectly matches who we are instead of working for a company that tells us what they think is the perfect job description for us ladies. You are smart, powerful and a creative human being. It is important to remember your worth each day as your transform the world!

Network with Me!

I look forward to your emails. Send in your employment testimonies, and share stories about the new network of people you have met because you decided to be strong and courageous and try something new.

Email me at *drtjacques@gmail.com.*

I also look forward to meeting women who are now in their dream careers and who would like to share the tips that helped guide them into a successful interview. I look forward to sharing your stories in my next guide!

For booking inquires contact: Fruitful Vision Enterprises, *fvisionenterprises@gmail.com.*

Made in the USA
Las Vegas, NV
04 April 2022

46816521R10026